COLORS OF

London

Thunder Bay Press
An imprint of the Advantage Publishers Group
5880 Oberlin Drive, San Diego, CA 92121-4794
www.thunderbaybooks.com

All notations of errors or omissions should be addressed to Thunder Bay Press, Editorial Department, at the above address. All other correspondence (author inquiries, permissions) concerning the content of this book should be addressed to AA Publishing, Fanum House, Basing View, Basingstoke, Hampshire, England RG21 4EA

ISBN-13: 978-1-59223-492-9
ISBN-10: 1-59223-492-5

Library of Congress Cataloging-in-Publication Data
Dailey, Donna.
    Colors of London / Donna Dailey.
        p.cm.
    ISBN 1-59223-492-5 (trade cloth)
    1. London (England)--Pictorial works. 2. London (England)--Social life and customs--Pictorial works. I. Title.

DA684.25.D35 2005
914.21'0486--dc22   2005048549

Printed in China.
1 2 3 4 5   09 08 07 06 05

COLORS OF

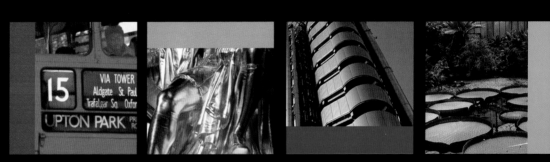

London

CONT

COLORS OF **LONDON**

INTROD

COLORS OF LONDON: **INTRODUCTION**

I came to London from the United States intending to stay for a few months and ended up living here for fifteen years (and counting). I quickly fell in love with the city, not only with its landscape but with its lifestyle. My London is a city of corner pubs, ethnic restaurants, strolls along the Thames, parties on the riverboats, brisk walks through sprawling parks, moments of retreat in small peaceful squares, browsing in antiquarian bookstores, finding bargains in the bustling markets, splurging on something special in a fashion boutique.

There is always something here to feed the senses and an inquiring mind: a fascinating exhibition of art or history, a new play or concert. But most of all, I love London for itself. I feel grounded in its rich history, uplifted by its continual surprises and endless possibilities. In large ways and small, it is a city of constant spectacle.

London is, of course, world famous. It even has a biographer, British novelist Peter Ackroyd, who has called the city "a living, breathing being." And London is indeed like a person. It has its good days and its bad. Its moods swing from bright to dark, animation to churlishness; and to really enjoy its company, you have to learn to ride those waves.

London is, by turn, amusing and exasperating. Its character is full of quirks and traditions, which have become as familiar as those of an old friend. As Ackroyd puts it in his masterwork *London, the Biography* (2000), "London is so large and so wild that it contains no less than everything."

The World's Marketplace

The heart of London is the River Thames, which has pumped its lifeblood through the city since ancient times. The Romans founded the city along its banks in the first century AD, and from its beginnings it has been, first and foremost, a place of commerce. The great tidal river, which enabled trade with the continent of Europe and later the world, was the key to London's prosperity. In the ninth century, the great Christian historian the Venerable Bede recorded that London was "the mart of many nations resorting to it by land and sea."

And it is still all about the money. People come here, as they have always done, to seek their fortune, to walk the legendary gold-paved streets. Today the City—the financial heart of the country and the biggest business center in Europe—is the domain of bankers and stockbrokers. They conduct their business in the same square mile as the first traders of Roman times. Leadenhall Market, one of the great city markets that can trace its roots to earliest times, stands on the site of the old Roman Forum. A Roman amphitheater lies beneath the Guildhall, the meeting place for the medieval craftsmen and merchants' guilds.

Here in the City, London retains its medieval street plan. Street names like Cornhill and Ironmonger Lane recall the original trades once practiced here. Although the old thatch and timber buildings are now replaced by brick and concrete, I can still feel the aura of the ancient marketplace underlying the modern city.

Urban Renewal

You won't see many traces of London's origins today, at least not on the city surface. Over the centuries, new generations have demolished and built over London's ancient past. Although much has been lost in the incessant need for expansion, you can peel back layer upon layer of the city's intriguing history in what remains. While the city's architectural treasures—from its beautiful churches to the grand buildings of the Georgian and Victorian eras—are impressive in themselves, it is their stories that bring them to life.

Renewal in London was often triggered by devastating events. In the Great Fire of 1666 and the blitz of World War II, much of the city was razed to the ground. Each time, London rose from its ashes with an amazing spirit of revival.

Today, London's rejuvenation stems from its soaring prosperity. The old wharves and warehouses of the Docklands, which once brought the city its commercial wealth, are now prime pieces of capital in themselves, reborn as trendy riverside apartments and office buildings. Newcomers to the city skyline, the bullet-shaped "Gherkin" and City Hall, are wrapped in shiny curves of glass and steel.

The Great Wen

In the early 1800s, the journalist William Cobbett called London "the all-devouring Wen," *wen* being an Old English word for a growth on the skin. During Cobbett's century, the city grew at lightning speed, from a population of one million in its first decade to nearly seven million by 1901. It became the world's largest city, its first great metropolis.

At the start of the new millennium, though no longer the biggest city on the planet, London's population has topped seven million and it sprawls over six hundred square miles. And how do Londoners get around this great urban space? Like it or loathe it, most use the Tube, London's underground system.

London led the way in public transportation with the opening of the world's first underground railway, which later became the Metropolitan Line, in 1863. The voracious Wen soon swallowed up

Millennium Bridge spans the Thames near the Tate
Modern art gallery to the south and St. Paul's
Cathedral to the north. When the pedestrian-only
bridge opened, it swayed alarmingly, but after
remedial engineering work it is now a popular
river-crossing point.

vast swaths of the surrounding countryside. Many of the stations on the Underground lines are the names of separate villages that stood there not so long ago.

A Dynamic Blend

From its beginnings, London was populated by migrants, and today it is as much a cosmopolitan world city as a national capital. It is home to a vibrant mix of people from all corners of the globe. There are nearly forty different ethnic groups here, each with populations of ten thousand or more. Some come from the former colonies and Commonwealth countries. Most come for the same reasons people have always flocked to the city: for the opportunity to work hard and prosper.

They have made London a dynamic city, giving it an exciting blend of foods, fashion, and culture. In a different quarter of the city, someone London-born and -bred is as likely to wear a sari or a *chador* as hipster jeans or a business suit. My favorite dining spots are just as likely to be a Turkish kebab establishment in Islington, a North African café in Shepherd's Bush, or a curry house in Brick Lane as an upscale restaurant in Kensington or the West End.

Walk along any main street in the city, and within a few minutes you'll hear an assortment of languages. Among the chatter of London accents, some talk "posh," some cockney, and others

Chinatown is centered on colorful Gerrard Street in Soho and houses lively and popular shops, supermarkets, and restaurants.

"mockney"—a somewhat snide label for the de rigueur affectation of the working-class accent considered essential to social success these days. Looking and sounding cool in London today is about attitude, not origins.

Now these rainbow faces are not foreign, but familiar. When I've been away from the city for a while, perhaps to the countryside or a more homogenous place, I'm happy to return to London's variety, to merge again into the great blend of humanity.

Landmarks

Even after many years in London, I still feel a quiet thrill at passing the city's grand landmarks. If I had to pick just one favorite, it would be Big Ben at night, lit up in the greenish-gold glow of its spotlights, shining like a beacon over the Thames. The sight of it as you drive along the Embankment, or across Westminster Bridge, never fails to lift the heart.

The river itself is London's most ancient landmark, and it threads together many of the city's greatest sights. Anchoring either end of the city's center are two of London's oldest monuments, the Tower of London and Westminster Abbey, the cores of which were built in the eleventh century.

St. Paul's has an even older pedigree. Although the present cathedral was built after the Great Fire of 1666, it is the fifth to stand on this site since the seventh century. Its magnificent dome is a symbol of the city, and the best view of it in all of London is from the river. In fact, until the building of the Millennium Bridge, the only way to see it from that angle was on a riverboat cruise. Even though the bridge offers such stunning views, I still take my visitors on the sightseeing boats,

because taking to the river is the best way to experience the essence of London.

We cruise beneath London Bridge, the city's only bridge across the Thames until the mid-eighteenth century. I picture it in medieval times, lined with nearly two hundred stores and houses, and with the severed heads of traitors stuck on pikes over the southern gate. Its latest concrete incarnation seems drab compared to the more ornate bridges spanning the river today, especially next to the Victorian flamboyance of Tower Bridge.

Another juxtaposition of old and new is nearby on the South Bank. The re-created Shakespeare's Globe recalls, for me, all the spectacle of Elizabethan London. The conversion of a defunct power plant into a splendid new home for the Tate Modern art gallery captures once again London's imaginative powers of renewal.

The most impressive sight on the Thames is the London Eye—not of the Eye itself, but from it. Riding in the glass pods as the big wheel revolves slowly above the river gives a whole new perspective on the city.

A Treasure House

London is a treasure house for much of the nation's finest art, from icons to Impressionists. A visit to the National Gallery, with its superb collection of Western European art from 1250 to the 1900s, is like a lesson in art history. Next door, famous figures in British history come to life at the National Portrait Gallery. These are among the more than seventy museums in the capital with free admission. Everyone can share in London's great cultural cache.

The British Museum is a showcase of world culture, with fascinating objects, from the temples of ancient Egypt and Assyria to Celtic treasures from nearer home. The Victoria and Albert Museum, named for the royal couple who aimed to bring culture to the masses, is a magnificent storehouse of decorative arts from around the world. Smaller but no less impressive are the superb displays of art at Somerset House or the Wallace Collection, or the curious collection of, well, everything at Sir John Soane's Museum in Lincoln's Inn Fields, the heart of London's legal district.

London is also the capital of BritArt, the confrontational, often iconoclastic contemporary works by the so-called Young British Artists. Although shock value often seems to be the main point, many YBAs are less controversial and have been accepted into the capital's mainstream. Photographer Sam Taylor-Wood has exhibited at the Hayward Gallery, while sculptor Rachel Whiteread created a sculpture for the empty plinth at Trafalgar Square.

Cool Britannia

Since the 1960s, when the world's hottest music came from the recording studios of Abbey Road and the coolest fashions were found on Carnaby Street and the King's Road, London has been a buzzword for everything hip. In the late 1990s, it suddenly became cool to be British, and London revived its title as the capital of Cool Britannia. A new confidence and energy gleamed from its shops, restaurants, bars, and nightclubs. In all things creative—theater, film, music, art, architecture, design, food, and fashion—London stands at the cutting edge.

Paris may be the home of couture, but London is the capital of style. The city has long been

The futuristic glass cars on the London Eye (opposite) offer an unrivaled view over the city as they slowly follow a full circuit of the big wheel.

famous for its classic tailoring, from the bespoke craftsmen of Savile Row to the high-fashion houses of Bond Street and Knightsbridge. A Burberry revival has made the venerable company's trademark gray-and-tan check raincoats, skirts, scarves, and bags hip as well as classic.

But London is best known for its quirky street fashion and the creativity of its young designers. London Fashion Week, held twice a year, is the launching pad for Britain's hottest new talents. John Galliano, Alexander McQueen, and Stella McCartney are among those who have made their names in the international fashion world, injecting new life into haute couture heavyweights like Gucci and Christian Dior.

London's hip street and club scene has inspired Paris couturiers such as Jean-Paul Gaultier and Christian Lacroix. If you want to get a jump on the next big trend, forget the stores of the West End. Head for the market booths of Spitalfields, Camden Lock, and Portobello Road, where budding designers flaunt their creations.

The City as Muse

Charles Dickens, London's most famous chronicler, claimed that the city was his muse. He often walked for miles across the city, finding inspiration for his stories and characters. It was the "magic lantern" that lit up his imagination, giving us a view of London that still captivates readers today.

I, too, prefer London on foot. No matter how often I walk familiar paths, I always notice something new, not just because London is always changing, but because it is so full of detail that you can't take it all in at one time. The multilayered images of the buildings that line the city streets, and the vibrant flow of people among them, are what makes London such a fascinating place, a place I never grow tired of.

If you travel only by Tube, popping up from area to area, you never get a sense of London's parts in relation to each other. But if you walk, say, from Islington to Clerkenwell, down through Bloomsbury to Covent Garden and the Strand, you will get a feel for how these once-separate villages have been stitched together to form the immense quilt of the city.

On my walks through the city, I have found my own London landmarks beyond the grand monuments and the great temples of art and culture. These are the places that capture the small beauties and eccentricities that make London such a special city. In winter, I like to wander through Waterlow Park up on Highgate Hill in north London, to see the enormous black bust of Karl Marx looming through the fence in Highgate Cemetery next door. In summer, I stroll along the Thames at Hammersmith, admiring the elegant, wisteria-covered houses of Chiswick Mall and ending up on the tiny riverside terrace of The Dove, a pub some four hundred years old. There are endless corners of London that reveal similar charms and take me back to an earlier time.

Dickens's London muse was a dark creature, rising out of mists and shadows, wrapped in a cloak of thick, gray fog. But if London were a woman, she would wear red, the color of her icons, the old phone booths and mailboxes, the double-decker buses and guardsmen's tunics. And she would wear green, the color of her vast city parks and leafy squares. She would wear the glorious colors of her flower gardens, the gaudy hues of her market booths. London is indeed a living, breathing being, and she wears every color of the rainbow.

FLAVORS

COLORS OF LONDON: **FLAVORS**

1

EATING OUT

Eating out is London's favorite pastime. Since the 1980s, when the city underwent a restaurant revolution, interest in food and new dining experiences has continued unabated. Food is hip. Food is fun. Countless column inches in the media are devoted to the hottest new cuisine and the places to see and be seen. Popular spots for sustenance and socializing are not limited to city-center restaurants such as those in Covent Garden (opposite top). The café at Somerset House (above) and the terrace at the Barbican complex (opposite right) are among many good places to eat out.

B ritish food used to have a poor reputation—but no longer. Today the flavors of London are among the great sensory experiences of the capital. You can watch the world go by over coffee and cake at a sidewalk table in summer or pass a rainy winter's afternoon in a cozy pub. Splurge on a gourmet meal cooked by one of the country's top celebrity chefs or enjoy a cheap and cheerful meal at a neighborhood trattoria. Have a traditional Sunday lunch (roasted meat, potatoes, vegetables, and gravy), breakfast at the local "caff," or taste your way around the globe via London's many ethnic restaurants.

To find the essence of London's flavors, visit the lively produce markets (overleaf), the city's chefs' source for fresh, quality ingredients for their culinary creations. Try Berwick Street in Soho, the organic markets at Spitalfields and Portobello Road, or east London's Ridley Road market for African and Caribbean fare.

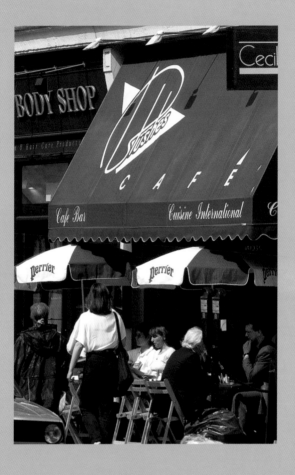

There are few more perfect London hours than one spent sitting in the sunshine at a sidewalk table. If the city's café life is less celebrated than that of Paris or Madrid, it is restrained only by the weather. When the sun comes out, Londoners grab every opportunity to indulge in a drink, a snack,

or a meal outdoors, where the passing scene provides continual entertainment. A ringside seat in Covent Garden, Soho (left), or the King's Road in Chelsea (center) puts you in prime people-watching territory.

London's passion for food is seconded only by its love of design. The old "greasy spoon" café has given way to bright, stylish coffee shops and brasserie-style cafés that often stay open into the late hours. Tradition is upheld by a handful of delightfully old-fashioned patisseries.

The coffee craze took London by storm. Chains from Starbucks to Costa have sprung up on every corner, and now workers arrive at the office with cappuccinos in hand. Neighborhood coffee shops, such as this Internet café in Brick Lane (above), are local gathering spots.

"There is nothing which has yet been contrived by man, by which so much happiness is produced as by a good tavern or inn." Samuel Johnson, the ultimate Londoner, wrote those words in 1776, but pubs (public houses) have been at the heart of London life since the Middle Ages. They are an integral part of British culture, and everyone has their favorite "local." Many pubs in central London have stood for centuries. Some, such as the Coach and Horses in Greek Street (bottom left), are well-known watering holes for writers and actors.

Nowadays, pubs cater to Londoners' discerning tastes in food and drink. Real ales and foreign bottled beers are popular, while dozens of independent breweries around the country produce distinctive beers that are drunk in the capital.

A good pub lunch—a steak and kidney pie, perhaps—is one of the simple pleasures of the city. But traditional pub grub has given way to fancier fare in "gastropubs," such as the Bleeding Heart Tavern in Clerkenwell (above), where meals rival those of high-quality restaurants.

The Pig and Whistle? The Frog and Nightgown? Britain's whimsical pub names are a source of great amusement, and London has its fair share. The colorful signs hanging outside many pubs date back to Roman times, when proprietors put stone reliefs outside their buildings showing a picture of their wares. An early Roman symbol for a tavern was an evergreen bush. In the fourteenth century, Richard II declared that all pubs must have a sign so the official ale taster could identify them.

Since most people were illiterate, pubs used simple pictures, such as the sun or a black swan.

Until the reign of Henry VIII, many had religious names like the Cross Keys, a symbol of St. Peter. Others, such as the Red Lion and White Hart, had royal links (to James I and Richard II, respectively). The seventeenth-century George Inn (top left) in Southwark is the only coaching inn left in London.

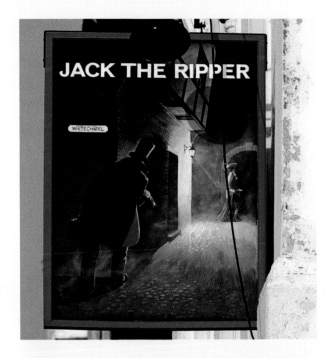

The most common pub name in the country is The Crown. The Victorian Dog and Duck in Soho (opposite top right) depicts a hunting theme, while the curiously named Fox and Anchor (top left) serves the market workers of Smithfield at 7 a.m. Many seemingly nonsensical names are corruptions of archaic or foreign names or phrases, thus Un et Chacun (One and All) became the Hen and Chickens. One of the longest pub names (bottom right) recalls the footmen of the eighteenth century who were hired by wealthy men to run in front of their carriages to remove obstacles and light the way.

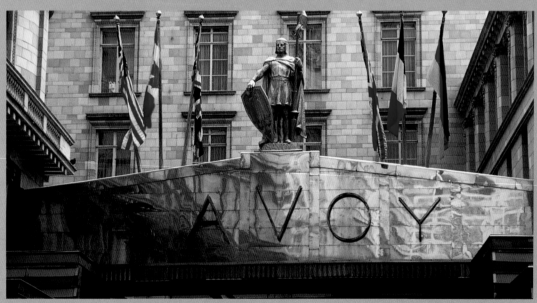

London's fine hotels are also the setting for classic dining in the capital. From the twenty-eighth floor of the Hilton on Park Lane, the contemporary French cuisine of Windows restaurant competes with the breathtaking views. At the Savoy, a quiet bastion of class and style, you can enjoy live music and lovely views of the Thames from the River Restaurant or visit the famous Savoy Grill, known as "the place where the deals are done."

With its exquisite gold chandeliers and striking trompe-l'oeil decor, the Ritz Restaurant is one of the most sumptuous dining rooms in London. The hotel is also the most glamorous setting in the city for afternoon tea (opposite), which is served in the beautiful Palm Court.

Rules in Covent Garden is one of London's oldest restaurants, established in 1798. The author Charles Dickens often ate here, and it is still popular with actors and theatergoers. It is known for its traditional British fare, especially excellent game.

Set in the magnificent Michelin building in South Kensington, Bibendum's dining room is as outstanding as its food and wines. Stained-glass windows show the Michelin Man in various poses, from riding a bicycle to drinking champagne.

It's only fitting that one of London's most prestigious hotels should have one of Britain's most famous chefs in charge of its restaurant. Superb food presented in stylish surroundings with impeccable service is the hallmark of Gordon Ramsay at Claridge's.

Reservations are made months in advance for a table at The Ivy in Covent Garden's theater district. It has long held cult status as one of London's top celebrity restaurants. The brasserie-style dishes are based on British favorites cooked with Continental and Asian accents.

Restaurant Gordon Ramsay at Royal Hospital Road in Chelsea is the flagship of the gourmet London dining spots run by this top British chef. The haute cuisine is rich yet light, presented with impressive service and style.

Chic, sleek Le Caprice, set discreetly behind the Ritz in Piccadilly, is another haunt of the rich and famous. Classic international dishes are served in the black, white, and chrome dining room decorated with portraits by celebrity photographer David Bailey.

Perhaps more than any other factor, the influence of ethnic cuisine has transformed London into one of the world's most exciting food capitals. French patisseries such as Maison Bertaux and Patisserie Valérie (top left) have served Soho for more than a century. But today, the cuisines brought by immigrants from around the globe are enjoying a new popularity. London boasts some of the best Indian restaurants outside the subcontinent, where you can sample distinctive regional dishes. Chinese dim sum houses, Italian trattorias, Spanish tapas bars, Greek tavernas, Turkish kebab houses, Japanese noodle bars, and restaurants featuring Polish, Thai, Malaysian, North African, and Caribbean food spice up the capital's dining scene.

ETHNIC INFLUENCE

While ethnic restaurants can be found throughout this multicultural city, some areas are particularly renowned for certain cuisines. Many Chinese restaurants are located in Soho's Chinatown, while Brick Lane in Spitalfields has more than forty curry restaurants serving everything from Kashmiri to Bangladeshi dishes. Southall is another good area for authentic Indian cuisine. London's East End is home to many immigrant groups, and along main streets like Kingsland Road, you'll find an eclectic range of restaurants serving Vietnamese, Turkish, and other ethnic fare.

LIFE & PE

OPLE 2

COLORS OF LONDON: **LIFE & PEOPLE**

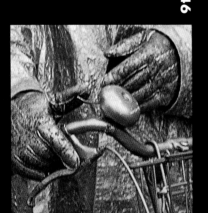

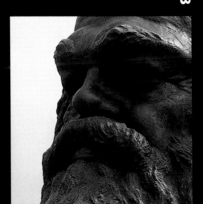

OFFICIALS

London's bobbies are world famous, and still refreshingly firearm-free. Police sometimes patrol the streets on horseback, especially in the royal quarter of St. James's. And No. 10 Downing Street, the home of the prime minister, must be the most famous address in Europe.

On the streets of London you'll see a rainbow of faces and hear a babel of languages from every corner of the globe. Above all else, it's the people who make London such an interesting city. They bring color and vibrancy to the drab backdrop of sidewalks and walls, and new blood into the traditional life of the capital.

It would be hard to describe a typical Londoner these days. Any stereotype that springs to mind is likely to be a face from the past, for today's capital is dynamically cosmopolitan. It's a wonderful mixture of the cultured and the bohemian. One of the most delightful things about London is that, in the midst of all its sophistication and cool, you will come across touches of quintessential Englishness that make it unlike any other city in the world.

ON THE STREETS

Many time-honored traditions still live on the streets of London. If you want to vent some verbal steam, head for Speaker's Corner (left) at the northeastern edge of Hyde Park. Here anyone can step up on a soapbox and sound off on religion, politics, and social issues ranging from animal welfare to smoking—and banter with hecklers in the crowd. Speaker's Corner has been a living testament to free speech since the right of public assembly was granted here in 1872.

London beat America by more than a century with the first shopping mall—Burlington Arcade— a covered promenade on Piccadilly built in 1819. It is still watched over by Beadles, former soldiers from the Tenth Hussars regiment. Dressed in top hats and frock coats (right), they prevent singing, whistling, and other infringements of the original Regency code of courtesy.

But London forges new traditions, too. In 2000, the water jets installed in the courtyard of the venerable Somerset House (left) were the first major public fountains to grace the city since those in Trafalgar Square in 1845.

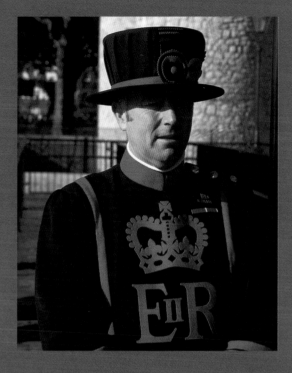

Oyez, oyez, oyez! The call to "hark" or "listen" dates back to the Battle of Hastings, when the first town crier spread the word of William the Conqueror's invasion in 1066. Peter Moore (top left) has been London's official town crier for more than twenty-five years.

Uniforms are the literal threads of London's history. They link not only the wearer but everyone who sees them with the city's glorious past. The Yeoman Warders, or "Beefeaters" (top right), who have guarded the Tower of London since the early fourteenth century, are a symbol of the city. Their

curious nickname may have come from their daily ration of meat: twenty-four pounds of beef, eighteen pounds of mutton, and sixteen pounds of veal for the thirty men on duty in 1813.

Red coats and bearskin hats are a handsome sight at the changing of the guard outside Buckingham

UNIFORMS

Palace (opposite right). Commissionaires (bottom
right) stand watch over the Bank of England.
   Chelsea Royal Hospital was founded by Charles II
in 1682 to provide for wounded and aged soldiers.
The red coats and tricornered hats of the Chelsea
Pensioners (right) are a lovable sight in the borough.

All the world's a stage—or at least, all the piazza. Every day Covent Garden is the scene of the best free show in town as its cobbled square becomes an open-air stage for mimes, magicians, acrobats, jugglers, clowns, comedy troupes, and a host of eccentric street performers.

The piazza's theatrical roots go back centuries. Its architect, Inigo Jones, was a stage designer who loved Italian architecture, and he built the piazza in the 1630s. Jones also built the church of St. Paul, the actor's church, with its portico along one side of the square.

The diarist Samuel Pepys recorded London's first Punch and Judy puppet show here in 1662, performed by an Italian puppeteer. Today, you should grab a ringside seat on the balcony of the Punch and Judy Pub overlooking the square for the best view of the entertainment.

STREET PERFORMERS

Street performing is actually illegal in London, but the Covent Garden Market has obtained a special license from the city. The performers have to audition for their pitch, and for most it is their full-time job. So if you like the show, be generous when they pass the hat.

In London's many statues and memorials you'll find a living history book of faces from the past. Royalty is well represented, particularly Queen Victoria. Her statue stands outside Kensington Palace, while her white marble monument (above) fronts Buckingham Palace.

Charles I (top right) lost his head to the executioner outside the Banqueting House in 1649, but it has returned in the form of a bust outside the building where he met his fate. The artist James Mallord William Turner (bottom right) is one of several artists honored in St. Paul's Cathedral.

Famous foreigners are also remembered in London. The enormous bronze head of Karl Marx (opposite left) tops his grave in Highgate Cemetery. The statue of Mahatma Gandhi (opposite right) is the focus of the peace garden in Tavistock Square.

MAHATMA GANDHI
1869 — 1948

Sometimes every street in London seems to have a historical connection. Throughout the city, blue plaques commemorate famous people who lived or worked in the buildings where they are displayed. The first plaque, marking the birthplace of Lord Byron, was erected in 1867 outside 16 Holles Street. Today there are over 760 plaques honoring writers, artists, actors, politicians, scientists, economists, and others who have made a contribution to human welfare or happiness. You'll find them in all parts of the city, and they reveal many surprises about who once called London home. The top five visited plaques are rated as Sherlock Holmes (despite his fictional status), John F. Kennedy, Charles Dickens, Karl Marx, and John Logie Baird (the Scottish engineer who made television possible).

221b
SHERLOCK
HOLMES
CONSULTING DETECTIVE
1881–1904

SIR
JOHN
BETJEMAN
1906 – 1984
Poet Laureate
lived here

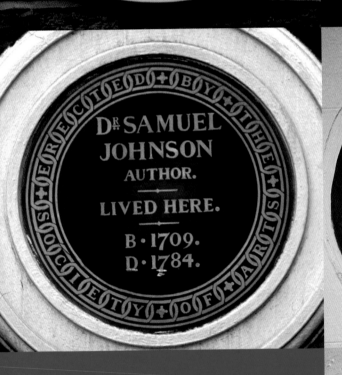

Dr SAMUEL
JOHNSON
AUTHOR.

LIVED HERE.

B·1709.
D·1784.

GREATER LONDON COUNCIL

JOHN
MAYNARD
KEYNES
1883–1946
Economist
lived here
1916–1946

ERECTED BY CAMDEN LONDON BOROUGH COUNCIL
HERE AND
IN NEIGHBOURING
HOUSES DURING
THE FIRST HALF OF
THE 20th CENTURY
THERE LIVED SEVERAL
MEMBERS OF THE
BLOOMSBURY GROUP
INCLUDING
VIRGINIA WOOLF
CLIVE BELL AND
THE STRACHEYS

HISTORIC HOUSE

GEORGE
ORWELL
1903 – 1950
NOVELIST & ESSAYIST
LIVED AT 27B
1945

LONDON BOROUGH OF ISLINGTON

50

LCC

BENJAMIN DISRAELI
Earl of
Beaconsfield
Born Here
1804

NELSON.
LIVED HERE in 1797.
—
BORN 1758.
FELL at TRAFALGAR
1805.

GREATER LONDON COUNCIL

WILLIAM
MARSDEN
1796-1867
SURGEON
Founder of the Royal Free
and Royal Marsden
Hospitals
lived here

SIR
WINSTON
CHURCHILL
Lived in a house
on this site
1921-1924

LONDON COUNTY COUNCIL

SIR
HENRY
IRVING
1838 - 1905
ACTOR
lived here
1872-1899

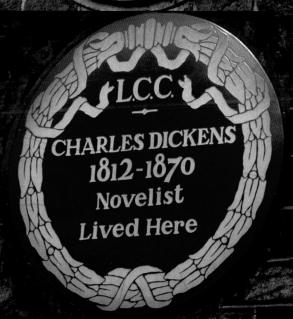

L.C.C.

CHARLES DICKENS
1812-1870
Novelist
Lived Here

NELSON'S COLUMN

You'll need binoculars for a closer look at one of London's most famous historical figures—Admiral Horatio Nelson—high atop his column in Trafalgar Square. The statue, guarded by four bronze lions, commemorates Nelson's victory against the French at the 1805 Battle of Trafalgar.

As well as being Britain's naval hero, he also plays unofficial host every year to New Year's Eve revelers, who gather at his feet to celebrate as midnight approaches.

ARCHITE

CTURE 3

COLORS OF LONDON: **ARCHITECTURE**

CHURCHES **66**

MODERNIST **68**

BRIDGES **72**

DETAILS

As befitting of one of the world's greatest cities, London has a magnificent array of architecture. A roll call of the capital's most famous buildings is like a walk through history: the White Tower built by William the Conqueror, Henry VIII's Tudor palace at Hampton Court, the Renaissance Banqueting House in Whitehall, Georgian squares, Regency terraces, the neoclassical Royal Exchange, and Victorian Gothic Law Courts. While some live out their retirement as popular visitor attractions, others remain an integral part of business and public life in London.

"Everywhere in this city the past and present are locked in a mysterious embrace," observes London's biographer, Peter Ackroyd. "Every journey through its streets becomes a journey to the past."

In the oldest parts of London, such as the City or along the Thames, the spirit of the past is palpable. As you wander through ancient lanes and courtyards, let your imagination transport you back in time. Picture the people, their clothing, and their trades, the sounds and smells that once enveloped the place you now pass through. Peel back the invisible layers, and London's architecture becomes much more than mere bricks and mortar.

To truly appreciate London's architectural treasures, you must pay attention to details. It's easy to become enthralled with the grand spectacle of the great cathedrals and monuments, but often the small touches are the most delightful. You may spot an interesting sundial or clock on the ornate facade of a church; whimsical weather vanes top the Royal Mews and Liberty and the Art Nouveau store in Regent Street. Look for gilded figures on important public buildings and gilt leaf on palace gates. Other details on mosques and embassies depict London's international community.

VERDIGRIS

To see some of London's most interesting architectural features, just look up. Step aside from the stream of traffic and pause for a moment. Let your eyes wander skyward, and you will often discover a completely different world.

Many of the lovely Queen Anne–style houses along Pont Street in Knightsbridge are topped by Dutch gables and terracotta decorations (top left). Renovations aim to enhance the characteristics of London's historic public buildings. When the Royal Opera House in Covent Garden was refurbished in the 1990s, it incorporated the iron-and-glass structure of Floral Hall, a nineteenth-century flower market, into a magnificent foyer (bottom left). Architect Terry Farrell used a similar feature, albeit in a postmodernist style, in his design for Charing Cross Station, rebuilt in 1991 (opposite left).

Copper domes, turrets, and cupolas top many public buildings constructed in the Victorian era, such as the ornate central tower of Smithfield Market (opposite right). Weathering created the greenish-blue substance called verdigris that forms on copper and brass. The enormous domes of the Byzantine-style Westminster Cathedral (right), the country's principal Roman Catholic church, are overshadowed by its bell tower.

If you're wondering why little remains of medieval London, the answer is fire! In the early hours of September 2, 1666, a fire broke out in a bakery in Pudding Lane. Wind carried the sparks to neighboring buildings, and by morning London Bridge was in flames. The fire quickly spread

BRICK

through London's tightly packed, thatch-roofed wooden houses. It raged for four days, destroying four-fifths of the city, including more than thirteen thousand homes and forty-four livery halls. As the city rose from its ashes, an edict was proclaimed. London would be rebuilt in brick and stone.

The Great Fire set the stage for the building of London's handsome Georgian terraces (opposite) and squares. The Victorians favored red brick for housing developments, often used to great effect in gables (top right) and other decorative features. The old Tudor chimney stacks at Hampton Court

(bottom right) and the mock-Tudor chimneys of Liberty (top left) are some of the most interesting brickwork in London. Bright new brick developments are springing up on every available space (above left) to fill the demand for housing in the crowded capital today.

London's biggest event in Victorian times was the Great Exhibition of 1851. All the wonders of the age in industry and technology were displayed in Sir Joseph Paxton's Crystal Palace, itself a grand piece of engineering. The building was 1,850 feet long and 110 feet high, tall enough to incorporate the huge elm trees that stood on the original site in Hyde Park. With its iron structural frame and glass walls, it looked like a giant greenhouse. It inspired the use of these materials in many other Victorian buildings, particularly market halls and train stations. One of the finest examples, Leadenhall Market (above and opposite left), stands on the site of the old Roman Forum, its traders selling meat, fish, and produce as they have done here for over two thousand years.

VICTORIAN

The Victorian years also saw a revival in Gothic architecture. You can spot Gothic arches and details not only in churches and public buildings but also in this collision of architectural styles that adorn these ornate Victorian buildings of Eastcheap (right).

London has always been a city of churches. By the twelfth century, around one hundred parish churches had been built within the city walls. London's largest medieval church is also the most famous religious building in Britain: Westminster Abbey (left). It was built between 1050 and 1066 by Edward the Confessor, who died only a week after its consecration and became the first king to be buried there. It is as much a national shrine as it is a place of worship, the coronation place of the country's monarchs, and the burial place for many of its most famous figures.

London's other great landmark, St. Paul's Cathedral, has an even longer history. The first St. Paul's was built here in 604. The Norman Old St. Paul's, built in 1087, stood for nearly six hundred years until it was destroyed in the Great Fire of 1666, along with eighty-six London churches.

CHURCHES

Sir Christopher Wren, the architect of the new cathedral, also designed fifty-two other churches to replace those that were lost. Unfortunately, nearly a third of these were destroyed by bombs during World War II.

MODERNIST

Modern architecture is like modern art: everyone has an opinion, not always flattering. While some people see modernist architecture as incongruous among the city's Victorian and Regency grandeur, others see it as a symbol of London's dynamic growth, its forward place as a world leader.

The 1980s set a tidal wave of transformation in motion, and it continues today. Half of all the office buildings in the City were rebuilt in just eight years, bringing shiny new creations like Sir Richard Rogers's Lloyd's of London building (opposite) onto the skyline.

The latest newcomers are City Hall, a distinctive sphere of glass where the mayor of London and the London Assembly reside (above), and the Swiss-Re headquarters, a bullet-shaped glass tower designed by Sir Norman Foster and affectionately known as the Gherkin.

Way out

The greatest rejuvenation was seen in the Docklands area, where a new center of commerce and industry was created on the site of unused docks along the Thames. Its showpiece is One Canada Square, better known as Canary Wharf Tower (opposite right). With its completion in 1990, it became the tallest building in the United Kingdom at 771 feet, surpassing the NatWest Tower (opposite left), which had held that title for the previous decade. Canary Wharf even has a futuristic underground station (above).

Around three million people lined the banks of
the Thames on New Year's Eve 2000 to celebrate
the arrival of the twenty-first century with a
spectacular fireworks display. London also splurged
on several millennium projects to add beauty and
culture to the city.

One of these was the Millennium Bridge
(above), the first pedestrian bridge to be built
across the Thames in more than a century.
The bridge links the city's oldest landmark,
St. Paul's Cathedral, with its newest, the Tate
Modern art gallery.

BRIDGES

Pictures on page 73, clockwise from top left: Tower Bridge, Albert Bridge, Westminster Bridge and the Houses of Parliament, Hungerford Bridge and Hammersmith Bridge

LANDM
& VIE

What is a London landmark? It's the Tower, the Thames, and the great royal palaces, to be sure; it's the abbey, the cathedral, and dozens of splendid parish churches. It's a world-class museum or gallery and a world-famous department store; Big Ben and Madame Tussauds. Once you've seen the memorials to the great and the good, seek out the landmarks of ordinary Londoners: the bustling markets, the parks and gardens, the corner pubs where the business of life goes on much as it has for centuries. London is not a city of skyscrapers. Most of its tallest buildings are office towers, not tourist attractions. But you can still find bird's-eye views from the dome of St. Paul's, the bell tower of Westminster Cathedral, Tower Bridge, or the capital's latest landmark, the magnificent London Eye.

MARKETS

From its beginnings, London was a trading city. For centuries, goods were sold in a dozen markets, including Smithfield for meat, Billingsgate for fish, and Covent Garden for fruit and vegetables. Some of these markets are still thriving, and they've been joined by many more all over the city today.

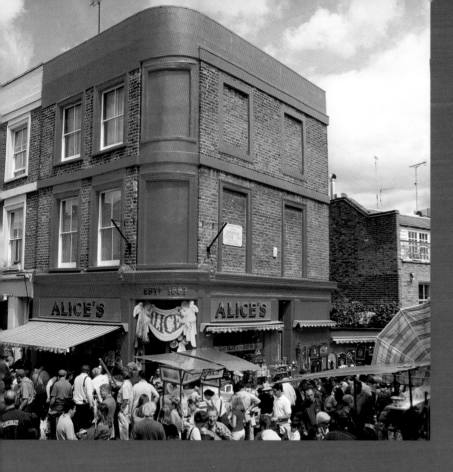

Portobello Road is famous for antiques, and for the celebrity faces spotted browsing its burgeoning stalls. London's foodies flock to Borough Market on Fridays and Saturdays, and Spitalfields on Sundays, for two of the capital's best organic produce markets. Look for leather jackets and cheap designer fashions in Petticoat Lane. Camden Town is mobbed on the weekend with hip young things seeking trendy clothing and accessories. And Covent Garden, although no longer a market, is always a big draw with its great variety of arts, crafts, and entertainment.

Going green? Welcome to one of the world's greenest cities. Greater London has 1,700 parks, encompassing seventy square miles. You can chill out in quiet, shady squares dotted throughout the city or get some exercise striding across the great expanses of Hampstead Heath or Hyde Park.

You can even walk the two miles through the heart of the city from Westminster to Notting Hill and never leave parkland. Londoners have royalty to thank for some of their finest green spaces. In the 1660s, Charles II opened St. James's Park, formerly a royal deer park, to the public and strolled the grounds with his mistresses. Richmond Park, Greenwich Park, and Hyde Park are royal parks to this day. Giant water lilies, soaring palms, and tropical flora are among the plants that flourish in the magnificent greenhouses of Kew's Royal Botanic Gardens (opposite).

Throughout the grounds, there are species from every habitat around the globe. In the city center, Londoners indulge their passion for flower gardens in Holland Park, Regent's Park, and Kensington Gardens.

There are wonderful stories behind some of London's most famous landmarks. The much-loved statue of Peter Pan in Kensington Gardens (top left) was erected in the dark of night on April 30, 1912, so that its magical arrival would greet people strolling through the park on May Day morning.

Cleopatra's Needle, an ancient Egyptian obelisk, was presented to Britain in 1819 by the viceroy of Egypt, Mohammed Ali, but for many years it was too heavy to ship. In 1878, it was finally floated to London. The sphinxes (bottom left) that flank it are Victorian re-creations.

London's most famous statue, erected in 1893, is the figure of Eros (opposite center), which tops the bronze fountain at Piccadilly Circus at one end of Shaftesbury Avenue. The sculptor, Sir Alfred Gilbert, created the winged archer not as the god of love but as the Angel of Christian Charity to commemorate the philanthropist, the Earl of Shaftesbury. The statue of Achilles (opposite right), the ultimate warrior, stands in Hyde Park as a memorial to the Duke of Wellington; it was cast from the cannons that gave him victory in so many of his battles with Napoléon. The Celtic warrior queen Boudicca rides her chariot on the Victoria Embankment (top), and the four-horse chariot driven by the Angel of Peace stands on top of the Wellington Arch, in the corner of Hyde Park (above).

LONDON EYE

For the millennium, London got a new landmark and a new view. Many feared the Eye would be an eyesore, but this giant observation wheel soon won over its critics. A slow ride in one of its glass pods provides a stunning view. It lets you see the city and its buildings from a new perspective.

PARLIAMENT

One of the most famous symbols of London is the Houses of Parliament and its Clock Tower (officially called St. Stephen's Tower), which houses the famous Big Ben. The tower was built after a fire destroyed the old Palace of Westminster in 1834.

with its symmetrical towers and pinnacles, stand on the south side of Westminster Bridge and look at it from across the Thames. You might see its reflection shimmering in the water or capture its grand silhouette at sunset. Big Ben is the thirteen-

around the world on daily broadcasts from the BBC. No one knows exactly how it got its name. It may have been named after the works commissioner Sir Benjamin Hall, who supervised the clock's installation in 1858, or the heavyweight

BUCKINGHAM PALACE

TOWER OF LONDON

The Queen's London residence, Buckingham Palace (previous page), is a world-famous symbol of monarchy and the focus for ceremonial and public occasions. Originally Buckingham House, a duke's country mansion, it only transformed into a royal palace after George III snapped it up in 1761.

In contrast, the Tower of London can trace its royal lineage back almost one thousand years, serving as armory, fortress, and residence. The nightly Ceremony of the Keys has hardly changed in more than seven hundred years.

ST. PAUL'S CATHEDRAL

St. Paul's is Britain's only domed cathedral, with one of the world's largest domes, second only to that of St. Peter's in Rome. Even today, despite towering office blocks, the great dome remains one of the distinctive outlines of London's skyline. The Whispering Gallery runs round the dome's interior. Here, acoustics are such that someone standing on the opposite side of the gallery can hear your whispers quite clearly after several seconds' delay—though only early visitors have the peace to test the theory properly. Dizzying views (above right) can be seen from the Golden Gallery, at the highest point of the dome. A hole in the floor also gives a mesmerizing glimpse down to the cathedral floor.

ART CULTURE & STYLE

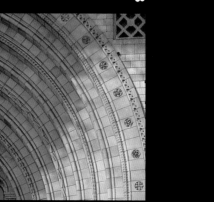

Art, culture, style—it would be hard to find three better words to sum up what makes London such an exciting city. On the one hand, London culture is tradition: royalty and red coats, pomp and circumstance; on the other, it's pop and punk, Bond Street and Savile Row, Top Shop and "Harvey Nick's." The cosmopolitan population of the capital also creates a dynamic blend of culture and style that makes it like no other city. London has some of the finest art galleries in the world, and the city continually inspires a new generation. A community of artists around ten thousand strong—the largest in Europe—thrives in Shoreditch, Hoxton, and other parts of east London. From media to advertising, theater, film, and music, the city is bursting with creative talent.

Some images of London are famous all over the world. But are London's icons under threat? The familiar red phone booths have largely been usurped by modern silver and Plexiglas models. New flexible buses are replacing the old double-decker Routemasters in many parts of the city.

Even the traditional red mailboxes may go, because the postal service may soon face competition from private mail-delivery companies.

ICONS

London is the stage for all of Britain's great state occasions. Royal ceremonies take place every day in the capital, from the Changing of the Guard at Buckingham Palace to the Ceremony of the Keys at the Tower of London, where a Yeoman Warder locks the gates each night with a military escort.

Guardsmen with bayonets and bearskin hats keep watch over the royal palaces 24-7.

The most spectacular event, Trooping the Colour, takes place the second Saturday in June, when the queen rides down the Mall in a horse-drawn carriage as dozens of horse guards and foot

guards and a military band parade in honor of her official birthday. The royal coach also carries the monarch to the State Opening of Parliament each fall. And cannons still fire in royal salute in Hyde Park to commemorate royal anniversaries and special occasions.

PAGEANTRY

It's hard to imagine London without the pageantry that connects the capital to centuries of British history. Today, many people question the role—and cost—of the monarchy in the modern world. Should it ever be abolished, London's ceremonies would be reduced to nothing more than staged re-creations; but for now, they remain an integral part of the country's culture and tradition, thrilling millions of visitors and residents with their spectacle.

London's great shopping temples are tourist attractions in themselves, particularly the city's luxury department stores. Fortnum and Mason on Piccadilly was founded by a former footman at Buckingham Palace, William Fortnum, and his landlord, Hugh Mason. It prospered due to its royal connections and developed a reputation for gourmet foods. It was possibly the first purveyor of fast food in the form of ready-to-eat delicacies like poultry and game topped with seafood.

Harrods, which now sells everything from Burberry coats for dogs to toy Humvees, also began as a humble grocery and tea store in 1849. Today its motto is "everything for everyone, everywhere," but its heart lies in its seven lavish food halls (above), where you'll find more than 300 cheeses, 60 salamis, 150 varieties of bread, 100 kinds of fish, and, of course, 150 different teas.

Art meets fashion in another London landmark, Liberty, on Regent Street (above). Founded by Arthur Lasenby Liberty in 1875, it expanded from selling Oriental rugs and textiles to creating its own opulent fabrics and distinctive designs for which it is known today.

"The customer is always right," according to Henry Gordon Selfridge, the American who created London's first custom-built department store. It opened on Oxford Street in 1909 with a library, a soda fountain, and even a "silence room," where women shoppers could relax. Selfridges first promoted the concept of shopping as fun. Today, with its ritzy design, music, and lighting, shopping here is an ultramodern experience.

GALLERIES

Two highly contrasting venues stage many of the top temporary exhibitions in the capital. The concrete bunker that houses the Hayward Gallery on the South Bank (opposite top right) and the Palladian mansion of Burlington House, now home to the Royal Academy of Arts. The latter became the country's first formal art school in 1768, and two of its first students were the painters John Constable and Joseph Turner. You don't necessarily have to be a master to show your work here. The Academy's Summer Exhibition is open to all the country's artists, amateur and professional alike. Each year about a thousand works are chosen for display, and all are for sale. The most intimate art experiences take place in London's smaller galleries, such as the Wallace Collection and Kenwood House.

The former home of Sir Joshua Reynolds in Covent Garden now houses the superb Photographers' Gallery (above left). Even the café is a work of art at the Serpentine Gallery in Kensington Gardens, which hosts fascinating changing exhibitions from around the world.

The Saatchi Gallery on the South Bank is the home of BritArt, the work of the so-called Young British Artists, or YBAs, some of whom aren't so young anymore! It began in 1988 with an exhibition in a Docklands warehouse with the work of young conceptual artists assembled by BritArt's

most famous star, Damien Hirst. More than a decade later, outrageous and provocative are still its hallmarks—think Hirst's dead cow in a fish tank, or Tracey Emin's unmade bed.

MODERN

TATE

A renovated power plant on Bankside became the celebrated venue for London's newest gallery, the Tate Modern. Its opening in May 2000 provided a massive exhibition space for the Tate's collection of international modern art and allowed its gallery of British art to spread out at its Millbank location, now called Tate Britain. The old Turbine Hall is a huge dramatic space for large installations, while the upper floors house themed exhibits and changing exhibitions.

NATURAL HISTORY MUSEUM

Where can you see the world's largest mammal (the blue whale), a 1,300-year-old giant sequoia, and a life-size tyrannosaurus rex under the same roof? The galleries of the Natural History Museum pay homage to the awesome variety of life on earth, from the smallest insect to the largest dinosaur.

By mid-Victorian times, Britain's growing empire and seafaring explorations around the globe had sparked a public fascination with the natural world, so plans were laid for a museum that would showcase the wonders of the plant, animal, and mineral kingdoms. It opened in 1881 with

thousands of specimens from the collections of Sir Hans Sloane and Sir Joseph Banks, who sailed with Captain Cook on his first voyage around the world in the 1760s. Today the museum holds more than sixty-five million specimens and over a million books and manuscripts.

THE ROYAL ALBERT HALL

One of the great events of London's cultural calendar is the Henry Wood Promenade Concerts—known as the "Proms"—which are held in the Royal Albert Hall each summer. The music ranges from classical to modern, but the last night always ends with great emotion as patriotic songs are played.

Few London buildings portray the continuity of time as well as Shakespeare's Globe. The original theater was built in 1599 by Cuthbert and Richard Burbage, helped by the rest of their acting company, one of whom was William Shakespeare. In 1599, the Privy Council, enraged by the content of some of the plays being written by London dramatists, closed all the theaters in the city of London, so the Globe relocated to Bankside, on the south side of the Thames, outside the city walls. In 1613, during a production of *Henry VIII*, the Globe caught fire and burned to the ground. It was swiftly rebuilt, but in 1642 Oliver Cromwell's government closed all theaters with an act of parliament, and, shortly after, the Globe was destroyed.

THE GLOBE

More than three hundred years later, American actor and director Sam Wanamaker came to London and was shocked to find that nothing of the theater remained. He spearheaded a campaign to reconstruct the Globe, as closely as possible to the original.

Shaped like an O, the theater is made of oak timbers and white plaster walls held together by oak pegs instead of nails. It has the only thatched roof allowed in London since the Great Fire. Plays are performed in the open air, using the afternoon light, just as they were in Shakespeare's day.

LIGHT &
REFLECT

COLORS OF LONDON:
LIGHT & REFLECTIONS

IONS

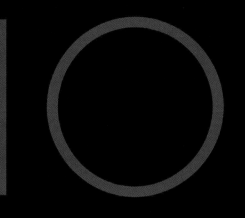

BRITISH MUSEUM

London isn't known as a city of lights, which makes the lustrous features it does display all the more striking. Because the skies are frequently clouded with gray or rain, when the sun does come out it's simply magic. Dull brick buildings shimmer with red and yellow hues as if freshly painted; even drab concrete and metal structures sparkle under a blue sky. Nowhere is the effect more dazzling than on the Thames. To stand in the center of one of its bridges, looking upriver and down at familiar landmarks set against a sunny sky or reflected in the water, is to breathe in one of the most exciting vistas of the city.

Sir Norman Foster's magnificent canopy of glass curves over the Great Court of the British Museum has created an uplifting space of light and air where there once was darkness. Until the redesign and opening of the Great Court in 2000, this area had been a maze of storerooms; now it is Europe's largest covered square.

London's medieval buildings had dark interiors, with wood timbers and paneling and hammerbeam roofs. But in the early seventeenth century, Inigo Jones (1573–c.1672) cast architecture in a new light with his neoclassical Renaissance buildings, inspired by his travels in Italy. Jones gave England its first

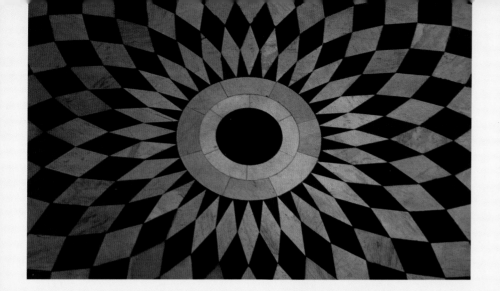

INTERIORS

Palladian building, the lovely Queen's House, built at Greenwich (1616–1635) as a rural retreat for Queen Anne of Denmark, wife of James I. The finest feature of its interior is the spiral Tulip Staircase (opposite), named for the flower pattern on its balustrade. Jones's other great masterpiece in central London, the Banqueting House, was described as "the model of the most pure and beautiful taste" by the author Horace Walpole. These buildings were the prototypes for many of the country's stately homes and public buildings. In the latter part of the eighteenth century, some of London's great houses were remodeled by the architect Robert Adam (1728–1792), who gave them elegant neoclassical interiors with statuary, decorative plasterwork and marble floors. These include Kenwood House, Osterley Park House (above), and Syon House.

London is the theater capital of the world. There are more theaters here than in any other city, and you can see popular musicals like *The Phantom of the Opera*, Shakespeare's plays, comedies, dramas, monologues, or avant-garde productions nearly every night of the week.

ornate Victorian decor. At night, London basks in the neon glow of the West End, the nucleus of London's theater district.

The blueprint for today's theaters was the original Theatre Royal in Drury Lane (left). Oliver Cromwell closed down all theaters in

mid-seventeenth century, and this was the first to receive a royal charter when Charles II reopened them in the 1660s. Here, the actor David Garrick revolutionized the theater with elaborate scenery, sound effects, and, above all, lighting. Imagine the darkened stage illuminated only by hundreds of

candles, reflected in tin backings designed to magnify their glow. This was one of the illusions Garrick devised to produce the kind of spectacle that thrilled his audience and kept them coming back for more. His techniques elevated theater from a lowly profession to the glittering success it remains today.

FILM

ODEON WEST END

FANATICAL ABOUT FILM

There are no brighter stars in London than those of the big screen. Britpack actors, such as Jude Law, Keira Knightley, and Ewan McGregor, are taking Hollywood by storm. British writers and directors are behind some of the biggest hits of recent years, including Anthony Minghella's *Cold Mountain*, Peter Webber's *Girl with a Pearl Earring*, and Richard Curtis's *Love Actually*. The homegrown film industry is thriving too, with over $2.1 billion spent on UK productions in 2004.

The big, glitzy movie theaters of the West End are as glamorous as the stage theaters for a night on the town, and Londoners line the edges of Leicester Square to get a glimpse of the stars who turn out for British film premieres. On the South Bank, the National Film Theatre (opposite top) is the focus of the annual London Film Festival in late October and early November, while London's IMAX cinema (above) has the biggest film screen in the country.

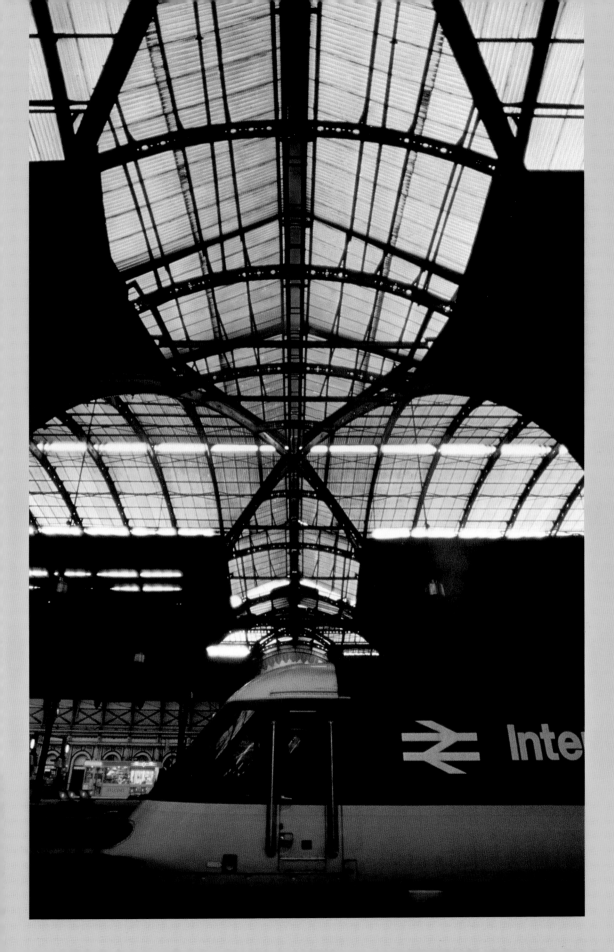

GLASS

From the stained glass of its historic churches to the glass walls of its modern office buildings, London reflects the light. The graceful terminal of Paddington Station (left) was designed from 1850 to 1854 by Isambard Kingdom Brunel, the leading engineer of the Victorian era.

THAMES

London would not exist without the Thames. Its name derives from *tamesis*, an ancient Celtic word for river, a name the Romans kept when they founded their city here in the first century AD. This great tidal river once made London the most important port in the world and was the lifeblood of the city until well into the twentieth century. Today the Thames is largely a place of recreation. You can cruise eastward through about thirty miles of Greater London, from the palace at Hampton Court to the Thames Barrier (above) at Woolwich Reach.

For centuries, there was only a single bridge across the Thames. The old London Bridge was lined with stores and houses, which were not removed until the mid-eighteenth century when two new bridges were built at Blackfriars and Westminster. Today there are many more river crossings. Some, such as Tower Bridge (overleaf) and Albert Bridge (top left), are ornate attractions in themselves. Others provide vantage points for the illuminated landmarks of London, from the glowing face of Big Ben to the massive reflections of the Tower.

Tower Bridge is a London landmark and, as well as serving as a passage across the Thames, its hydraulically operated bascules allow tall ships to pass below. The bridge is still lifted more than nine hundred times each year

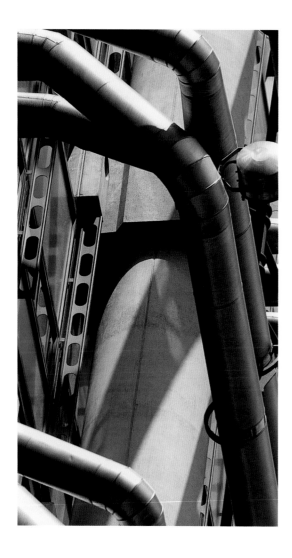

Possibly the most famous building constructed in the latter part of the twentieth century was the Pompidou Center in Paris. But London has an "inside-out" building, too. The Lloyd's Building (above) in the City was designed by Sir Richard Rogers, one of the cocreators of the Pompidou.

When it opened in 1986, this fourteen-story tower of steel, aluminum, concrete, and glass was both exciting and controversial, standing amid one of London's most traditional quarters. Ventilation shafts and stairways snake up along its exterior walls, alongside suspended cubes and cylinders.

It looks eerily futuristic at night, glowing with green and purple spotlights. Ironically, this space-age office block was built for one of London's oldest institutions, the insurance underwriters Lloyd's of London, whose business began in a small coffee shop in the seventeenth century.

METALLIC

A less successful rendition of modern architecture is the South Bank Centre, designed and built in the 1960s and 1970s. It is controversial for different reasons. On the one hand, it houses London's premier performing arts complex, with spacious venues for music, dance, art, and theater.

On the other, the gray bunkerlike buildings are seen as unfriendly and unattractive. A facelift for the entire complex is on the cards, though city planners have yet to agree on a new design. Still, with its superb riverfront plaza and walkways, much can be forgiven.

TIME & MOTION

TRAIN TRANSPORTATION **138**

BLACK CABS **136**

ILLUMINATION **134**

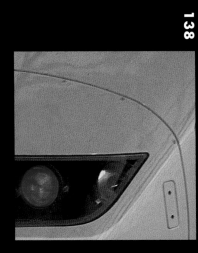

BUSES **140**

MOTION **142**

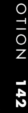

ILLUMINATION

In the beginning was the Thames. The river flows through the heart of London, marking time, a watery lifeline from the founding of the city on its banks to today's eastward expansion into the rejuvenated Docklands and beyond. Riverfront landmarks such as the Tower of London have stood here for centuries, watching the great rush of activity from dawn till dusk, guarding the city through the night. They anchor the capital through its many layers of history, connecting past and present. London is a city always in motion, and while time never stands still here, if you pause and reflect in an atmospheric corner, you will feel its ancient rhythms. Steel and concrete may replace wood and brick, but the timeless flow of human activity on this patch of earth is immutable.

There are 20,000 black cabs in London, and an average of 31,000 people looking for a ride, so cabdrivers have to move fast. Since 1851, they've been required to take an exam to on the best routes around the streets—it's called the Knowledge.

London's Underground system, also known as "the Tube," is the oldest and most extensive network of its kind in the world. The 500 trains and 160 stations certainly present a challenge when it comes to maintenance, because much of the track is old and subject to repairs. The stretch of track between Waterloo and Bank, in the heart of the business center of the capital (top left), is known as the "Drain" and is heavily used during rush hours. The latest additions to the network are the computerized, driverless trains of the Docklands Light Railway (right), which serve the

TRAIN TRANSPORTATION

revived Docklands area and the east of the city. For those looking to travel to continental Europe, the most civilized way to travel is by Eurostar (above). The two-hour journey from London to Paris takes passengers through the Channel Tunnel, which was featured in the movie *Mission Impossible*.

BUSES

London's bright red double-decker buses, along with the black cabs, have become a London icon. Hop on the back of an older-style Routemaster bus to be greeted by the conductor, and enjoy the view from the top deck while moving around the city at a more measured pace.

MOTION

Londoners beat the traffic by bicycle or motorbike
on the city streets, from commuters to couriers.
Take a shortcut through one of London's green
parks and you'll also find a rush of in-line skates
or gliding skateboards, used for sport and
transport alike.

CREDITS

The Automobile Association wishes to thank the following photo libraries for their assistance with the preparation of this project:

Photodisc 4bl, 18br, 27bc;
Trade Mark of Transport for London 97bl
London Underground Roundel.

The remaining photographs are held in the Automobile Association's own photo library (**AA World Travel Library**) and were taken by the following photographers:

Peter Baker 82r; **Stuart Bates** 70l, 73tl, 115br, 130c, 130r; **Theo Cohen** 79c, 128; **Barry Gendler** 78l; **Debbie Ireland** 60bl; **Richard Ireland** 14r; **Max Jourdan** Front cover t, 5bcl, 6, 8/9, 12/3, 18l, 20c, 21tl, 22tr, 22cl, 22bl, 22br, 23tr, 23cl, 23bc, 23br, 25, 26bl, 36bc, 37bl, 38l, 38tr, 40r, 41l, 41r, 44bl, 45tl, 45bl, 46tl, 46tc, 46bl, 47l, 47r, 55bc, 57bl, 57tc, 71, 74bl, 74br, 76bc, 77tl, 77bl, 81tc, 81bl, 81br, 84, 85l, 85r, 95bl, 97bl, 98r, 99l, 102l, 102c, 102r, 103l, 103c, 103r, 104tr, 106l, 106r, 109, 114bl, 116/7, 120l, 121l, 121r, 122t, 122b, 123, 128/9, 133bl, 133bc, 136br, 140tl, 140tr, 141t, 141c, 142l, 142r, 142br, 143tl, 143bl, 143cr, 144; **Paul Kenward** 4br, 24r, 27ctc, 30tl, 54br, 56tl, 57tr, 57bc, 57br, 58bl, 58br, 59tl, 59c, 59r, 60tr, 61l, 62l, 63tl, 65l, 82bl, 82tl, 95br, 100c, 101l, 101r, 105l, 105tr, 105b, 110, 113, 127tl, 130l; **S&O Mathews** 119c, 138; **Simon McBride** 48l, 55br, 59br, 68, 72/3, 75bc, 88/9, 91l, 97bc, 97r, 104bl, 107, 134t, 134c, 134b; **Jenny McMillan** 42bl, 52cl, 94bc, 98bl, 99; **Michael Moody** 14l; **Robert Mort** Back cover r, 3tr, 11c, 17, 20tr, 21tr, 24c, 27bl, 44cr, 70r, 73bl, 76cl, 78l, 78r, 79r, 91ctr, 124, 132bl, 132bc, 135, 137; **Clive Sawyer** 73br; **Barrie Smith** Front cover main, 19bc, 26r, 32c, 36bl, 39, 46cr, 51cl, 66l, 73c, 86, 139; **Rick Strange** Back cover cr, 3tcr, 4bc, 11r, 19br, 28tl, 28tr, 34tl, 34c, 35cl, 36br, 37br, 38br, 43, 44tc, 44cl, 45tr, 45br, 50tl, 50tr, 50c, 50cb, 51tl, 51tc, 51cr, 51bc, 52tc, 53, 63bl, 69, 73tr, 74bc, 75bl, 80tl, 81cr, 82br, 83r, 87, 95bc, 96l, 108l, 108r, 110/1, 127tr; **James Tims** Back cover l, cl, 3tl, 3tcl, 10, 26tl, 30bl, 34tr, 35r, 48tr, 56tr, 57bl, 57tl, 80cr, 81tl, 92l, 92r, 93r, 96r; **Martin Trelawny** 29tl, 45c; **Richard Turpin** 50br, 54bl, 54bc, 56br, 58cl, 59bl, 60tl, 61r, 62r, 63tr, **Roy Victor** 5bl, 44 **Tim Woodcock** 80 27bcr, 28bl, 29bl, 52cr, 77tr, 90, 91c 140bl; **Peter Wilsc** 58r, 66r, 67r, 82tl **Wrona** 10/1, 94bl,